What folks are saying about "Uncle Eggbert's Egg Book"

"Eggbert Fowler is just the sort of eggs-pert egg-centric we need in these backyard chicken times. Let no egg (or 'yolk') be wasted!"

—Michael Perry, author of *Coop* and *Population 485*

"Every time I pick up this whimsical book, it puts a smile on my face. And the recipes are delightfully delicious too!"

— Mi Ae Lipe, author of *Bounty from the Box: The CSA Farm Cookbook*

"Delightful, quirky, and practical: Egg recipes for breakfast, lunch and dessert plus entertaining chicken-and-egg lore, all lavishly illustrated with vintage photographs."

—Susan Thurin, owner Bookends on Main

"Recipes, found art, wit, and wisdom ... all about eggs and chickens. This book's got it all."

—Lindsey Quinnies, The Local Store

"These nutritious and delicious, palate- and appetite-pleasing recipes (and so many more kitchen cook friendly egg-based dishes!) make 'Uncle Eggbert's Egg Book' a 'must' for personal, family, and community library cookbook collections."

—Wisconsin Bookwatch

"You'll want to keep this book out on the kitchen or coffee table—not on the shelf with the other cookbooks. The random facts, amusing photographs, and quirky illustrations keep the pages turning!"

—Tanya Young, home and private chef, Menomonie, Wis.

"Love and eggs are best when they are fresh."
—Russian Proverb

RECIPE INDEX

Boiled Eggs: Hard or Soft 7
Super-simple Scrambled Eggs 8
Old-Fashioned Fried Eggs 9
Kick-butt Deviled Eggs 11
Poached Eggs 12
Breakfast Burrito 14
Breakfast Pizza 15
Toad in the Hole 16
Egg Salad Supreme 17
Egg, Sausage, Biscuit Casserole 23
Egg & Ham Crescent Squares 24
Hash Brown Potato Pancakes 25
French Toast Supreme 26
Waffles 27
Baked Eggs in Hash Nests 28
Nice Little Nest Eggs 29
Mix-n-Match Omelette 32
Ham, Cheese & Broccoli Quiche 33
Crab Cakes 34
Salmon Patties 35
Cheesy Shrimp Eggchiladas 36
Egg & Cheddar Cheese Puff 37
Drop Noodles 39
Potato Gnocchi 40
Roasted Scalloped Corn 41
Fluffy Dumplings 42
Sausage-Stuffed Peppers 43
Egg Drop Soup 44

Potato Chip Chicken Tenders	45
Easy Meatloaf	47
Breaded Zucchini Planks	48
Breaded Pork Loin Chops	49
Cheesy Egg Casserole	51
Spanakopita (Greek Spinach Bake)	55
Tuscan Chicken Torta	57
Oven-Crisp Eggplant	59
Darn Near Anything Skillet Frittata	60
Mustard Potato Salad	62
Ham & Egg Mash-ups	63
Spamwich Spread	65
Spinach Bacon Salad	66
Pickled Beets and Eggs	69
Craizy Banana Applesauce Bread	71
Zucchini Bread	72
Fried Rice and Shrimp	75
Baked Custard	77
Lemon Meringue Pie	78
Strawberry Honey Omelette	80
Sunny Lemon Squares	83
Mile High Pound Cake	84
Classic Lemon Curd	85
Hummingbird Cake	87
Bread Pudding	91
Congo Bars	92
Old-Fashioned Blueberry Muffins	93
Homemade Tom & Jerry Eggnog	94
Flour-Free Monster Cookies	95

Henrietta's Henhouse Hints ... 102

Dear Reader:

Not long ago my husband Eggbert and I decided to get ourselves some backyard chickens. They started out as four tiny, little chicks that could fit into the palms of our hands. Before long, they were a friendly flock of three hens—Daisy, Bernadette and Cleo—overseen by Ollie, the proud rooster.

A few months later, we started to get some eggs, which was pretty exciting. Soon, we were having poached eggs for breakfast, hard-boiled eggs for lunch and fried eggs for supper. We gave eggs to family and friends—which they appreciated—but we quickly realized that we needed to expand our egg recipe repertoire.

So we began to collect and try out different recipes that used eggs. Eggbert decided to compile our favorite recipes, along with other interesting bits of wisdom and whimsey related to eggs and chickens.

We hope that you enjoy this book—and your backyard chicken adventures—as much as we've enjoyed putting it together.

—Henrietta Fowler

Boiled Eggs — Hard or Soft

Ingredients
- Eggs
- Salt & pepper to taste

Step 1: Place eggs in cooking pan and cover with cold water.

Step 2: Bring to a boil, then cover and remove pan from heat.

For Soft-Boiled Eggs...

Let egg sit in hot water about 3 minutes, then dunk it into cold water for a few seconds so it will stop cooking and be easier to handle. Crack egg over toast.

For Hard-Boiled Eggs...

Let eggs sit in hot water for about 12 to 15 minutes, then run them under tap water to cool.

Eggs cooked too long will look greenish at the edge of the yolk.

Tips & Tricks

- To make it easier to remove the shell from hard-boiled eggs, use eggs that are at least a week old.

- The easiest and most fun way to remove the shell from a hard-boiled egg is to drop the egg into a small jar, add about an inch of water, tighten the lid on the jar and shake vigorously for about 5 seconds. The shell will slide right off.

- To separate the yolk from the white, hit the egg sharply on the rim of a mixing bowl, insert your thumbs in the crack, and pull the shell apart, tipping it so that the white runs into the bowl and the yolk stays in one half of the shell. Drop the yolk into a cup or smaller bowl.

SUPER-SIMPLE SCRAMBLED EGGS

Ingredients
- 4 eggs
- 1 Tablespoon water
- Salt and pepper to taste

Step 1: Whisk together eggs, water, salt and pepper.

Step 2: Place in microwave-safe dish, cover loosely with a sheet of waxed paper, and cook on high for two minutes.

Step 3: Stop and stir eggs.

Step 4: Cook on high for about another one and a half minutes, until eggs are desired firmness.

NOTE: Microwave cooking times vary greatly, so you may need to do some experimenting to find the perfect cooking time.

Stovetop Alternative

Step 2: Pour egg mixture into oiled frying pan, stirring regularly with heat-proof spatula. When eggs begin to thicken, reduce heat and continue to fold them over. Cook until eggs are desired firmness.

Feeding the hens.

OLD-FASHIONED FRIED EGGS

Ingredients
- Eggs
- Salt & Pepper to taste

You can't beat a fried egg!

Step 1: Crack an egg into the frying pan and cook to desired firmness.

For that old-fashioned taste, first fry up some bacon, then use the same pan and fry the eggs in bacon grease.

How do you want your egg?

Sunny Side Up
Your egg yolk looks like a bright morning sun. Crack an egg directly into your greased frying pan, then fry it until the edges brown, without flipping.

Over Easy
You go from sunny side up to over easy by simply flipping your egg when the edges are brown.

Over Medium
Over medium is the next step after over easy: they're fried, flipped, and fried a little longer, enough to cook the whites through and brown the edges slightly.

Over Hard
Fried, flipped, and fried again – usually with the yolk broken – until both the white and the yolk are completely cooked. Just tap the edge of your spatula into the yolk or poke it with a fork before turning it over.

Kick-Butt Deviled Eggs

Ingredients
- 6 hard-boiled eggs, peeled
- 2 Tablespoons mayonnaise
- 1 teaspoon prepared horseradish
- 1 Tablespoon dijon mustard
- 1 Tablespoon pickle relish, drained
- Parsley flakes

Step 1: Cut the eggs in half lengthwise and remove the yolks.

Step 2: Mix the yolks with the mayo, horseradish, mustard and relish.

Step 3: Refill the eggs with the mixture. Sprinkle with parsley flakes.

Q: Who should you invite over if you have deviled eggs?

A: An eggs-orcist.

POACHED EGGS

Ingredients
- Eggs
- Salt and pepper to taste

Utensils
- Frying pan

Step 1: Put about an inch of water in the frying pan and bring to a boil.

Step 2: Break an egg into a saucer or custard cup, one at a time, then slip it into the gently boiling water.

Step 3: Reduce heat so that water doesn't boil over. Cook until egg is desired firmness. To speed up the process, you can spoon some of the boiling water over the top of the egg.

Step 4: Serve over toast.

"I worked as a waiter when I was 15 and got a chance to appreciate good, simple food. There's nothing better than a boiled egg with toast."

—Ewan McGregor

Q: Why did the game warden confiscate the cook's eggs?

A: Because they were poached.

Breakfast Burrito

Ingredients
- ½ pound bacon
- 5 eggs
- 1 can refried beans
- 1 medium tomato, cut up
- 1 cup shredded cheddar cheese
- 4 flour tortillas (10 inch)
- Salsa
- Sour cream

Step 1: Fry the bacon until evenly brown. Drain and set aside.

Step 2: Pan scramble the eggs (no water or milk needed).

Step 3: Heat the refried beans and warm up the tortillas.

Step 4: Spread the beans on the tortilla, then cover with one quarter of the bacon, eggs, tomato and cheese. Roll tortillas into burritos, top with sour cream and salsa. Serves four.

Should Eggs Be Refrigerated?

Backyard eggs that are fresh and have not been washed do not need to be refrigerated, as long as you are going to use them within a relatively short period of time.

According to the American Egg Board's Egg Safety Center, the shelf life for an unrefrigerated egg is 7 to 10 days; for refrigerated, 30 to 45 days. A simple rule of thumb is one day at room temperature equals one week under refrigeration.

Breakfast Pizza

Ingredients
- 1 pre-made deep-dish pizza crust
- 1 cup frozen hash browns, thawed
- ½ cup cut-up sweet peppers
- 1 cup fresh sliced mushrooms (4 oz.)
- 1 package brown-n-serve breakfast sausage, cut up (1 cup)
- 1 cup shredded cheese (cheddar or mozzarella)

- 5 eggs
- ¼ cup milk
- ½ teaspoon salt
- ½ teaspoon black pepper

Step 1: On the pizza crust, spread out the hash browns, peppers, mushrooms and sausage. Use a deep-dish pizza pan under the crust to avoid dripping in the oven.

Step 2: Beat together the eggs, milk, salt and pepper and pour over the other ingredients.

Step 3: Cover with the cheese.

Step 4: Bake in 400° oven about 25 minutes.

When pouring the egg mixture over the other ingredients, avoid letting it seep under the crust...
...it will make the crust stick to the pan.

How Safe are Eggs to Eat?

The CDC (Centers for Disease Control) reports that something less than ½% of all foodborne illness is related to eggs. According to the USDA, only one egg in 20,000 might be contaminated with Salmonella. Based on the USDA statistics, that means that the average person might eat a contaminated egg once in 84 years.

Toad in the Hole

Ingredients
- Eggs, 1 per serving
- Bread, 1 slice per serving
- Butter, about 1 Tablespoon
- Salt and pepper to taste

Utensils
- Frying pan or griddle

A fun and tasty variation is to cut a slice of bell pepper to create a ring in which to fry the egg.

Step 1: Cut a hole in the center of the bread. An empty soup can works well to punch out the hole.

Step 2: Place the bread on a hot, well-buttered griddle or frying pan.

Step 3: Break an egg into the hole.

Step 4: When egg has begun to set, flip it over. Salt and pepper to taste.

Egg Salad Supreme

Ingredients
- 6 eggs, boiled, peeled
- 2 Tablespoons mayonnaise
- 1 Tablespoon spicy brown mustard
- ¼ teaspoon salt
- ¼ cup chopped celery
- 1 Tablespoon pickle relish or chopped cucumber
- Black pepper to taste

Step 1: Chop eggs

Step 2: Mix in other ingredients

Step 3: Serve in bread or burger buns with lettuce

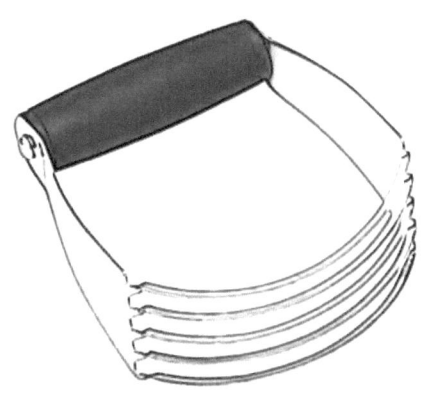

To easily chop eggs for egg salad, use a pastry blender in a round-bottom mixing bowl.

Can Eggs be Microwaved?

You can scramble, fry and poach eggs in a microwave, but you cannot cook an egg in its shell in the microwave. The steam builds up so rapidly that the egg cannot "exhale" it fast enough and the egg may explode.

Chickenology 101
by Old Bill

Chickenology is one of the most interesting of studies. Old Bill is Professor of Chickenology, and anyone who visits his place will hear wonderful things about chickens and their government.

Bill has studied chickens so long that he has discovered that every chicken run is a limited monarchy, ruled by the First Boss. The constitution is based on "He can take, who has the power; and he can keep, who can." The First Boss, like so many of our own political bosses, is a grafter, and he holds his power, like our bosses do, by careful division of the graft.

The first boss has to fight his way to the throne. For the first few months he and the other little cockerels run with the hen and the pullets. Then, when the little roosters are about six months old, they commence to fight among themselves. The chicken run is the scene of great battles. Each rooster pairs off with another one, and they fight and fight until one wins.

The victor immediately pairs off with another victor, and they fight. Every rooster must fight, and his standing depends on his strength. Eventually two of the little roosters beat all the others and then they fight until one wins. That one is the first boss, and the next one second boss.

The next year the boss of that brood fights the old boss, trying to displace him. It may take him two years, sometimes more, to become boss of all the yard, and then he may be beaten by some younger boss.

While he is boss, however, he rules the yard, taking the best of all the food, and distributing it according to his likes among the hens or his friends. Thus he holds his power until another boss beats him, and then he retires from active life and remains in quiet careers until condemned to be stewed.

Old Bill says chicken government is a good deal like our own and that the lot of the First Boss seldom is as happy as that of the ones who are beaten in the first round and are content with quiet and peace without seeking more power.

Picture and text reprinted from an 1890s stereoview card, publisher unknown.

Old Bill and His Happy Family.

EGGS SIZES AND EQUIVALENTS

4 Ex Lg eggs = 1 cup   5 Lg eggs = 1 cup
6 Ex Lg whites = 1 cup   7 Lg whites = 1 cup
12 Ex Lg yolks = 1 cup   14 Lg yolks = 1 cup

5 Med eggs = 1 cup   6 Sm eggs = 1 cup
8 Med whites = 1 cup   9 Sm whites = 1 cup
16 Med yolks = 1 cup   18 Sm yolks = 1 cup

SHOULD EGGS BE WASHED?

When an egg is laid, there is a protective layer over the shell called the cuticle that helps keep moisture in and bacteria out. To preserve this cuticle, it is best to brush or wipe the egg clean, if necessary, but not to wash it.

Egg, Sausage, Biscuit Casserole

Ingredients
- 1 pound sausage
- 8 eggs
- ¾ cup milk
- 1 can biscuits (grand size)
- 1 cup shredded mozzarella cheese
- 1 cup shredded cheddar cheese
- Salt & pepper to taste

This makes 8-10 servings. It reheats easily and freezes well.

Utensils
- 9" x 13" backing pan, greased

Step 1: Preheat oven to 425°.

Step 2: Brown sausage. Drain away any grease.

Step 3: Spread out biscuits to cover bottom of 9" x 13" pan.

Step 4: Spread sausage over biscuits.

Step 5: Mix together eggs and milk. Pour over sausage.

Step 6: Spread cheese over the top.

Step 7: Bake 30-40 minutes at 425°.

Egg & Ham Crescent Squares

Ingredients
- ¼ cup ham cubes
- 2 eggs
- 2 mushrooms, sliced
- 1 tube refrigerated crescent dinner rolls
- Cheese--a chunk of your favorite variety (this will be both cut into strips and grated)
- Salt & pepper to taste

Utensils
- Cookie sheet with edges

Step 1: Preheat oven to 400°.

Step 2: Unroll crescent rolls, being careful not to separate the triangles. Split into two square pieces (4 triangles each) and pinch together the seams.

Step 3: Cut strips of cheese and place them around the edge of each rectangle and then roll the dough over so the cheese is inside the edge of the crust and you now have basins with raised edges into which to put the eggs (stirred up) and ham.

Step 4: Top with mushrooms and a little grated cheese.

Step 5: Bake at 400° for about 18 minutes. Serves two hungry folks.

Zelda Fitzgerald, wife of writer F. Scott Fitzgerald, was asked in 1925 to contribute to "Favorite Recipes of Famous Woman." Here's her idea for making breakfast: "See if there is any bacon, and if there is, ask the cook which pan to fry it in. Then ask if there are any eggs, and if so try and persuade the cook to poach two of them. It is better not to attempt toast, as it burns very easily."

—"Careless People: Murder, Mayhem, and the Invention of The Great Gatsby" by Sarah Churchill

Hash Brown Potato Pancakes

Ingredients
- 2 eggs, lightly beaten
- 3 cups frozen shredded hash brown potatoes
- 2 Tablespoons flour
- 3 Tablespoons butter, melted
- 1 ½ teaspoon salt
- Olive or other cooking oil

Step 1: Rinse hash browns with cold water in strainer until thawed.

Step 2: Mix hash browns, eggs, butter, water and salt.

Step 3: Fry on hot, well-greased griddle, until golden brown on both sides. Makes 4 pancakes.

Q: What do you call an egg that goes on safari?

A: An eggs-plorer!

French Toast Supreme

Ingredients
- 4 eggs
- ½ cup milk
- 10-12 slices bread (my preference is oatmeal or multi-grain)
- 1 cup granola
- ½ teaspoon cinnamon
- Maple syrup

Utensils
- 2 flat-bottomed pans that will hold a slice of bread.
- Griddle
- Blender or food processor

Step 1: Grind up granola with cinnamon in a blender until it is the consistency of cornmeal. Put in one of the flat-bottomed pans.

Step 2: In a separate bowl mix together eggs and milk. Pour mixture into second flat-bottomed pan.

Step 3: Dip each side of a slice of bread into the egg mixture, then dip it into the granola crumbs to coat it.

Step 4: Fry on well-oiled griddle until golden brown and a little crunchy.

Step 5: Serve with pure maple syrup.

For best results, use bread that is a bit dry. If bread is very fresh, separate the slices and set them out on the counter to dry a little before using.

WAFFLES

Ingredients
- 2 cups flour
- 4 teaspoon baking powder
- 1 teaspoon salt
- 2 eggs, beaten
- 2 cups milk
- 3 Tablespoons melted butter

Utensils
- Waffle iron

Step 1: Thoroughly blend together flour, baking powder and salt.

Step 2: Add eggs, milk and butter, mixing thoroughly.

Step 3: Ladle onto waffle iron. Bake for about 4 to 5 minutes.

Baked Eggs in Hash Nests

Ingredients
- 4 eggs
- 1 can (15 oz.) corned beef hash
- 2 Tablespoons fine dry bread crumbs
- Salt and pepper to taste

Utensils
- 6" square baking pan

Step 1: Spread hash evenly in the baking pan. Form four depressions by pressing the bottom of a ½ cup measure into the hash.

Step 2: Break an egg into each depression, sprinkle with bread crumbs and salt and pepper.

Step 3: Bake at 375° for about 30 minutes or until eggs are as firm as you prefer.

Nice Little Nest Eggs

Ingredients
- 4 eggs
- 4 slices buttered toast
- ¼ teaspoon salt
- 2 teaspoons butter
- Pepper to taste

Utensils
- Baking sheet

Step 1: Preheat oven to 350°.

Step 2: Separate egg yolks and whites, keeping yolks for later use.

Step 3: Toast bread and butter, then place on baking sheet.

Step 4: Beat egg whites and salt until stiff and mound onto buttered toast slices.

Step 5: Make a well in the center of each mound of egg white, so it's like a little nest, and drop in the yolk. Top with ½ teaspoon butter.

Step 6: Bake at 350° for 15 to 20 minutes or until whites are lightly brown and yolks set. Pepper to taste.

A wife was cooking fried eggs for breakfast. Suddenly, her husband burst into the kitchen.

"Careful," he shouted, "CAREFUL! Put in some more butter! Oh my GOD! You're cooking too many at once. TOO MANY! Turn them! TURN THEM NOW! We need more butter. Oh my GOD! WHERE are we going to get MORE BUTTER? They're going to STICK! Careful! CAREFUL! I said be CAREFUL! You NEVER listen to me when you're cooking! Never! Turn them! Hurry up! Are you CRAZY? Have you LOST your mind? Don't forget to salt them. You know you always forget to salt them. Use the salt. USE THE SALT! THE SALT!!! THE SALT!!!"

The wife stared at him like he was crazy. She said, "What on earth is the matter with you? Do you think I don't know how to fry a couple of eggs?"

The husband calmly replied, "I wanted to show you what it feels like when I'm driving."

Mix-n-Match Omelette

Ingredients
- 6 eggs
- ¾ teaspoon salt
- Pepper as desired
- ⅓ cup milk
- 2 Tablespoons butter
- A: ¼ cup... (your choice)
    - ...sauteed sliced mushrooms,
    - ...sauteed sliced sweet peppers
    - ...black olives, sliced
- B: ¼ cup... (your choice)
    - ...cubed ham
    - ...cubed cooked chicken
    - ...breakfast sausage (cooked & drained)
- ½ cup cheddar cheese, grated

This makes two 3-egg omelettes. Split the ingredients between each.

Utensils
Large non-stick frying pan

Step 1: Beat eggs until yolks and whites are mixed.

Step 2: Melt butter in the pan, then pour in the egg mixture.

Step 3: Cook over moderate heat. As the omelette cooks, lift edges toward center and tip pan so that the uncooked mixture flows under the cooked portion. Continue cooking until egg is set.

Step 4: Place selected ingredient from A and from B and half the cheese on one side of the egg, then fold the other side over it and top with remaining cheese. Cook for about another minute or two and serve.

Q: What does a meditating egg say?

A: Ohmmmmmmmlet.

Ham, Cheese & Broccoli Quiche

Ingredients
- 6-8 eggs
- ¾ cup milk
- 1 cup chopped cooked ham
- 1 cup shredded cheddar cheese
- 1 cup chopped broccoli
- 1 deep-dish pie shell
- Salt and pepper to taste

For a tasty variation, substitute imitation crab chunks, mushrooms and swiss cheese for the ham, broccoli and cheddar.

Step 1: Pre-bake pie shell.

Step 2: Beat together eggs, milk, salt and pepper. Add ham and cheese.

Step 3: Pour mixture into pre-baked pie shell.

Step 4: Bake at 350° for 45 minutes.

Step 5: Let stand for several minutes before serving.

A man goes into a restaurant and is seated. An especially cute waitress comes to his table and asks, "What would you like, sir?"

He looks at the menu, then up at the pretty waitress and answers, "a quickie."

The waitress turns and walks away in disgust. After she regains her composure she returns and asks again, "What would you like, sir?" Again the man answers, "A quickie, please."

This time she asks the man to leave.

As he is walking out, quite puzzled by the waitress' response, a gentleman at the next table leans over and whispers, "Um, Pal, I think it's pronounced 'quiche'."

CRAB CAKES

Ingredients
- 2 Tablespoons butter
- 2 Tablespoons diced onion
- ½ cup bread crumbs
- 2 eggs, beaten
- ½ cup milk
- 2 cups cooked, flaked crab
- ⅓ cup diced celery
- ½ teaspoon mustard
- 1 teaspoon lemon juice
- 1 Tablespoon chopped parsley
- ½ teaspoon salt
- ½ teaspoon smoked paprika (regular will also work)

- 2 Tablespoons olive oil
- 1 cup flour

Imitation crab can also be used for this recipe.

Step 1: Melt butter in saucepan and saute onion and bread crumbs.

Step 2: Combine all ingredients except olive oil and flour. Chill for at least two hours.

Step 3: Shape into eight cakes, dust with flour.

Step 4: Fry cakes in olive oil for about eight minutes over medium heat until brown, turning once.

Salmon Patties

Ingredients
- 1 16 oz. can salmon, drained
- 2 eggs, slightly beaten
- ¼ cup finely chopped onion
- 1 Tablespoon flour
- 2 Tablespoons lemon juice
- ¼ teaspoon salt
- ⅛ teaspoon pepper
- 2 Tablespoons chopped fresh parsley
- 1 ½ cups crushed saltines (about 45 individual crackers)
- 3 to 4 Tablespoons butter

Step 1: Combine salmon, eggs, onion, flour, lemon juice, salt, pepper, parsley and 1 cup crumbs. Mix with fork until blended.

Step 2: Shape into 8 patties. Dip into additional saltine crumbs to coat.

Step 3: Fry at medium heat in well buttered skillet until crispy on outside (about 12 to 15 minutes).

Cheesy Shrimp Eggchiladas

Ingredients
- 1 medium onion, chopped
- 6 eggs, scrambled (see pg 8)
- ¾ cup salsa
- Shrimp, cooked, medium size, about 28
- 4 soft flour tortillas, 8"
- 1 cup grated pepper-jack cheese
- 1 cup grated sharp cheddar cheese
- 1 small tomato, chopped
- Salt & pepper to taste
- Sour cream
- Lettuce, shredded

Utensils
- 9" glass baking pan
- Frying pan

Step 1: Preheat oven to 400°.

Step 2: Fry the onions in a little olive oil and about a half cup of water until clear and carmelized. Set them aside, then use the same pan to scramble the eggs.

Step 3: Spread half of the salsa on the bottom of the baking pan.

Step 4: Fill the tortillas with the eggs, fried onions, shrimp and pepper-jack cheese, roll them up and place in the baking pan.

Step 5: Spread remaining salsa, chopped tomatoes and shredded cheddar cheese over the tortillas and bake at 400° for 15 minutes.

Step 6: Place eggchilada on plate, top with sour cream and shredded lettuce.

If you'd like potato cakes or rounds with this, they can be baked in the same oven at the same time and temp.

Egg & Cheddar Cheese Puff

Ingredients
- 3 tablespoons olive oil
- 1 medium onion, diced
- 2 red, orange or yellow bell peppers, seeded and cut into thin strips
- 3 cups (packed down) of shredded greens, such as kale or spinach
- Salt and pepper to taste
- 2 cups herb seasoned croutons
- 2 cups grated sharp cheddar cheese
- 12 eggs
- 3 cups milk
- 1 Tablespoon fresh thyme
- 1 teaspoon Hungarian paprika

This makes enough to feed a group ... and uses up a dozen eggs at the same time!

Utensils
- 9" x 13" baking pan
- Large skillet

Step 1: Preheat oven to 350°.

Step 2: In a large skillet, saute onions in olive oil, then stir in bell peppers, greens, salt and pepper, cover and cook for about 10 minutes, until peppers are softened and greens are wilted.

Step 3: Add bread cubes to sauteed vegetables, toss together and spread into 9" x 13" baking pan. Cover with 1 $1/3$ cup of the cheese.

Step 4: In a large bowl, whisk together eggs, milk, thyme and paprika.

Step 5: Pour egg mixture over the top of ingredients in the baking pan and then cover with the remaining $2/3$ cup cheese.

Step 6: Bake at 375° for 30 to 35 minutes, until eggs are set and top is golden brown.

"The key to everything is patience.
You get the chicken by hatching the egg, not by smashing it."

—Arnold H. Glasow

Drop Noodles

Ingredients
- 2 eggs
- 1 cup water
- 1 teaspoon salt
- 2 cups flour

Utensils
- 6 quart cooking pot

Step 1: Mix eggs, water and salt together in a large bowl.

Step 2: Add flour a little at a time, until it's a well-mixed dough. Set aside for about 30 minutes.

Step 3: Bring water to boil in large cooking pot

Step 4: Spread dough on a cutting board and cut it into bite-sized pieces, dropping them into the boiling water one at a time. Cook for five minutes after the last noodle is dropped.

Step 5: Drain in a large colander and rinse with cold water. Serve with sauce or soup.

Why are egg rolls called egg rolls if there's no egg in them?

It's because the dough for the egg roll wrapper is made with egg, flour, water and salt. Spring roll wrappers don't have egg in them. Neither should be confused with the annual White House egg roll.

Potato Gnocchi

Ingredients
- 2 potatoes
- 2 cups flour
- 1 egg
- ½ teaspoon salt

Step 1: Peel potatoes, cook until tender but still firm. Drain, cool and mash with a fork or potato masher.

Step 2: Combine 1 cup mashed potatoes, flour, egg and salt in a large bowl. Knead together until it forms a large ball.

Step 3: On a floured cutting board, shape the dough into two long snakes, each about a foot long. Cut snakes into ½ inch pieces. To add a bit of visual interest, press each piece gently with the tines of a fork.

Step 4: Bring a large pot of water to a boil. Drop in gnocchi, one by one, and cook for 5 to 7 minutes, until gnocchi have risen to the top. Drain and serve with butter or sauce. Makes about 48 pieces.

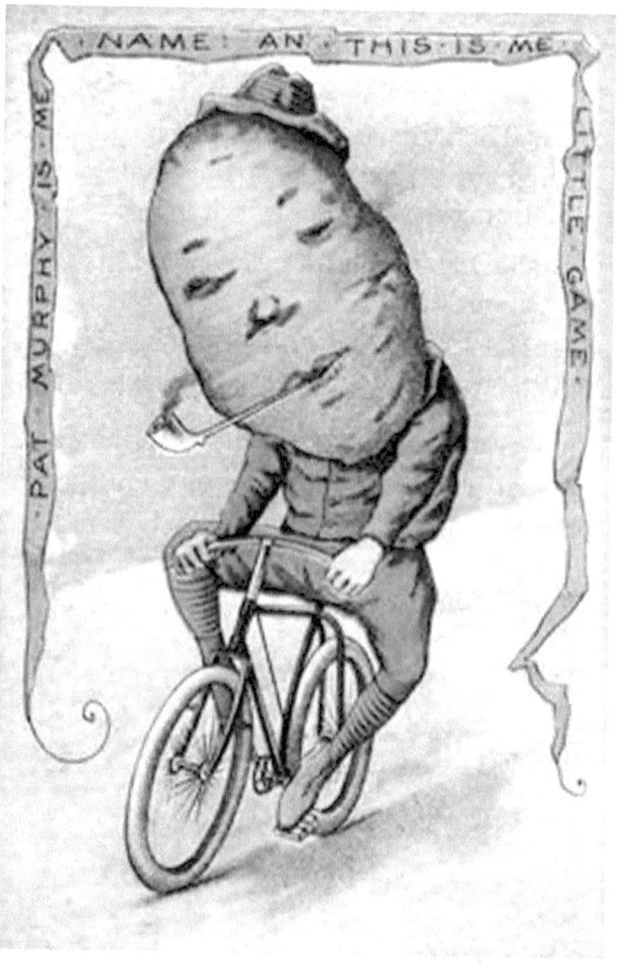

ROASTED SCALLOPED CORN

Ingredients
- 6 eggs
- 1 ½ cup milk
- ¼ cup butter
- 2 cups cracker crumbs
- 1 cup corn (frozen or canned, drained)
- ½ teaspoon grated onion
- 1 teaspoon salt (omit if using canned corn)

Step 1: Mix ingredients in order given.

Step 2: Let stand for 30 minutes, then pour into greased bread pan.

Step 3: Bake 30-45 minutes at 350°.

A Prize Ear of Corn

Eggs contain the highest quality food protein known. It is second only to mother's milk for human nutrition.

Fluffy Dumplings

Ingredients
- 1 ½ cups flour
- 2 teaspoons baking powder
- ¾ teaspoon salt
- 1 egg
- ½ cup milk

Step 1: Blend together flour, baking powder and salt.

Step 2: Beat egg until light and fluffy and add to dry ingredients.

Step 3: Stir in milk.

Step 4: Drop by tablespoons on gently boiling gravy, soup or stew. Cover tightly and cook for 15 minutes. *Tip: Don't open the lid midway to check the dumplings or they will quit rising.*

Sausage-Stuffed Peppers

Ingredients
- 4 large bell peppers
- 1 pound breakfast or Italian sausage
- ½ cup chopped onion
- 3 eggs
- ½ cup diced tomatoes, drained
- 1 cup cooked rice or quinoa
- ½ cup shredded mozzarella cheese
- 1 ½ cups marinara sauce

Step 1: Saute sausage and onions until browned. Drain.

Step 2: Mix together with eggs, tomatoes, rice and ½ cup marinara sauce.

Step 3: Fill hollowed-out peppers and top with cheese.

Step 4: Coat bottom of baking pan with ½ cup marinara sauce. Stand peppers in pan and pour remainder of sauce over them. Bake covered at 375° for about 55 to 60 minutes, until peppers are tender.

Egg Drop Soup

Ingredients
- 4 cups of chicken stock
- 1 Tablespoon corn starch
- ¼ teaspoon grated ginger
- 1 Tablespoon soy sauce
- 3 green onions, chopped
- ¼ teaspoon ground pepper
- ¾ cup sliced mushrooms
- 3 eggs, lightly beaten

Step 1: Stir together ½ cup of the chicken stock and the corn starch. Set aside.

Step 2: In a large pot, stir together the remaining stock, ginger, soy sauce, onions, pepper and mushrooms. Bring to a boil, then stir in the corn starch mix from step one and reduce heat to a simmer.

Step 3: Slowly pour in the beaten eggs while stirring the soup. The egg will spread out into ribbons. Turn off the heat and garnish with a few more chopped green onions. Serve immediately.

Potato Chip Chicken Tenders

Ingredients
- 3 split chicken breasts, thawed
- 2 eggs
- ¼ cup milk
- ½ cup flour
- ¼ bag crushed potato chips
- ½ teaspoon salt-free natural seasoning blend
- ½ teaspoon lemon pepper

This is a good way to use those left-over broken chips.

Step 1: Mix together eggs and milk.

Step 2: Mix together flour, potato chips, seasoning and lemon pepper and put into a paper bag (the empty chip bag works good for this).

Step 3: Cut up the chicken breasts into bite-sized pieces.

Step 4: Dip the chicken pieces into the egg/milk mixture, then drop the pieces a few at time into the potato chip bag and shake until covered.

Step 5: Place onto a baking sheet. Bake for about 25 minutes at 400°.

I'm having a great time in the country.

EASY MEATLOAF

Ingredients
- 1 ½ pounds ground beef
- 1 egg
- 1 medium onion, chopped
- 1 cup milk
- 1 cup dried bread crumbs
- Salt and pepper to taste
- 2 Tablespoons brown sugar
- 2 Tablespoons yellow mustard
- ⅓ cup ketchup

For a fun surprise when sliced, place a couple of hard-boiled eggs in the center of the loaf before baking.

Step 1: Preheat oven to 400°.

Step 2: In a large bowl, combine the beef, egg, onion, milk and bread crumbs. Season with salt and pepper to taste and place in a lightly greased loaf pan.

Step 3: In a separate bowl, combine the brown sugar, mustard and ketchup. Mix well and pour over meatloaf.

Step 4: Bake at 400° for about 50 to 60 minutes.

Breaded Zucchini Planks

Ingredients
- 2 medium zucchini
- Flour
- 2 eggs
- 2 Tablespoons water
- Bread crumbs, plain
- ¼ cup cooking oil

Utensils
- Large frying pan
- Flat pans for flour, egg mix, breading

Step 1: Wash zucchini and cut off ends. Cut lengthwise into ½" thick planks.

Step 2: Create an egg wash by mixing together the eggs and water.

Step 3: Coat both sides of zucchini with flour, dip both sides into egg wash, then coat both sides with bread crumbs.

Step 4: Put oil in frying pan. At medium heat, brown both sides of zucchini. When golden brown, set on paper towel to remove any excess oil. Salt and pepper to taste.

Q: How can you tell if a person has no friends?

A: She's in the grocery store buying zucchini.

Breaded Pork Loin Chops

Ingredients
- 4 pork loin chops
- 2 eggs
- ½ cup saltine cracker crumbs
- ½ teaspoon lemon pepper
- ½ teaspoon chopped chives
- ½ teaspoon basil
- ½ teaspoon salt-free natural seasoning blend

Step 1: Crush saltine crackers into crumbs and place in a flat pan. Mix in the lemon pepper, chives, basil and seasoning.

Step 2: Lightly beat the eggs in a flat bowl.

Step 3: Dip each chop in the egg mixture, then coat each side with the cracker crumbs.

Step 4: Bake at 410° on a lightly oiled baking pan for about 25 minutes.

Bake some potato wedges or french fries at the same time, for a simple all-at-once meal.

Cheesy Egg Casserole

Ingredients
- 2 cups (8 oz.) shredded Monterrey Jack cheese
- 2 tablespoons flour
- 1 cup (4 oz.) shredded sharp cheddar cheese
- ½ pound sliced bacon, cooked and crumbled
- 6 eggs
- ½ cup milk

Step 1: Toss Monterrey Jack cheese with flour and place in the bottom of a greased 8" x 8" baking pan.

Step 2: Top with cheddar cheese and sprinkle with bacon.

Step 3: Beat eggs and milk, then pour over the other ingredients.

Step 4: Bake uncovered at 325° for about 45 minutes, until a knife inserted in the center comes out clean. Let stand for a few minutes before serving.

This can be prepared the night before, refrigerated overnight, and then baked in the morning. Easy to double the recipe.

🥚 Frequently Asked Questions ...

Q: What happens when you make an egg laugh?
A: You crack it up.

Q: How do baby chickens dance?
A: Chick-to-chick!

Q: How do you know if it's too hot in the hen house?
A: The hens are laying hard-boiled eggs.

Q: Who tells the best egg jokes?
A: Comedi-hens!

Q: What do you call a mischievous egg?
A: A practical yolker.

Q: What sport are the eggs good at?
A: Running!

Q: What do chickens grow on?
A: Eggplants!

Q: Why do chickens lay eggs?
A: Because if they dropped them they would break!

Q: Why did the hen file a restraining order against the chef?
A: Because he beats her eggs!

Q: Why can't you tease egg whites?
A: Because they can't take a yolk!

... about Chickens & Eggs

Q: How did the egg get to the top of the mountain?
A: It scrambled up!

Q: How do comedians like their eggs?
A: Funny side up!

Q: What did Snow White call her pet chicken?
A: Egg White.

Q: What day do eggs hate most?
A: Fry-day!

Q: Why did the rubber chicken cross the road?
A: She wanted to stretch her legs!

Q: Why did the chickens quit laying eggs?
A: Because they got tired of working for chicken feed.

Q: Why did the chicken jump in the lake?
A: Because the rooster egged her on!

Q: Why did the chicken cross the playground?
A: To get to the other slide!

Q: What do you call a bunch of chickens playing hide and seek?
A: Fowl play.

A man walks into a bar with a fried egg on his head.

The bartender asks, "Why have you got a fried egg on your head?"

The man replies, "Because boiled eggs fall off."

Spanakopita (Greek Spinach Bake)

Ingredients
- 2 cups (16 oz.) ricotta cheese
- 1 package (10 oz.) frozen chopped spinach, thawed and squeezed dry
- 8 oz. crumbled feta cheese
- 6 Tablespoons flour
- ½ teaspoon pepper
- ¼ teaspoon salt
- 4 eggs, lightly beaten

Step 1: Combine the ricotta cheese, spinach and feta cheese. Add the flour, pepper and salt. Fold in the eggs.

Step 2: Spoon into a 9" lightly greased baking pan.

Step 3: Bake uncovered at 350° for about 45-50 minutes or until set. Remove from oven and let it sit for about 10 minutes before serving.

Eggs are placed in cartons with the large end up to keep the air cell in place and the yolk centered. Also, by storing eggs fat-end up, the pocket of air stays away from the yolk, and the egg stays fresh longer.

Tuscan Chicken Torta

Ingredients
- 1 ⅓ cups Bisquick baking mix
- 1 can (15 - 16 oz.) canellini beans, drained, rinsed and mashed
- ⅓ cup Italian dressing
- 1 ½ cups diced cooked chicken
- 1 package (10 oz.) frozen chopped spinach, thawed and squeezed dry
- 1 cup (4 oz.) shredded mozzarella cheese
- 3 eggs, lightly beaten
- 1 ¼ cups milk
- ¼ teaspoon salt
- ⅓ cup slivered almonds

Utensils
- 9" springform pan

Step 1: Combine baking mix, beans and dressing. Spread in bottom and two inches up side of ungreased springform pan. Bake at 375° for 10-12 minutes, until set.

Step 2: Layer chicken, spinach and cheese over crust.

Step 3: Mix eggs, salt and milk. Pour over cheese and top with almonds.

Step 4: Bake at 375° for 50 to 55 minutes, until golden brown.

Step 5: Let stand 10 minutes, then remove side of pan.

Note: Cannellini beans are large, white, Italian kidney beans.

> "It may be hard for an egg to turn into a bird: it would be a jolly sight harder for it to learn to fly while remaining an egg. We are like eggs at present. And you cannot go on indefinitely being just an ordinary, decent egg. We must be hatched or go back."
>
> —C. S. Lewis
>
> "A hen is only an egg's way of making another egg."
>
> —Samuel Butler

- Most eggs are laid between 7 and 11 a.m.
- Egg size and grade are not related to one another. Size is determined by weight per dozen. Grade refers to the quality of the shell, white, yolk and the size of the air cell.
- As hens grow older, they produce larger eggs.

Oven-Crisp Eggplant

Ingredients
- ½ cup fine cracker crumbs
- ½ teaspoon paprika
- ¼ teaspoon rubbed oregano
- ½ teaspoon salt
- 1 egg
- 1 Tablespoon water
- 1 medium eggplant
- ¼ cup melted butter

Step 1: Mix cracker crumbs with paprika, oregano and salt. Set aside.

Step 2: Beat egg with water.

Step 3: Peel eggplant and cut lengthwise into 6 segments.

Step 4: Dip eggplant slices into egg mixture, then dip into cracker crumbs.

Step 5: Place in shallow baking pan and drizzle with butter. Bake at 400° for about 25 minutes or until crisp.

Two Eggplants

One day two eggplants, who were best friends, were walking together down the street. They stepped off the curb and a speeding car came around the corner and ran one of them over. The uninjured eggplant called 911 and helped his injured friend as best he was able. The injured eggplant was taken to emergency at the hospital and rushed into surgery.

After a long and agonizing wait, the doctor finally appeared. He told the uninjured eggplant, "I have good news, and I have bad news. The good news is that your friend is going to pull through. The bad news: I'm afraid that he's going to be a vegetable for the rest of his life."

Darn Near Anything Skillet Frittata

Ingredients
- 3 Tablespoons olive oil
- ½ cup diced onions
- 8 eggs
- ½ cup milk
- ¾ teaspoon salt
- ¼ teaspoon pepper
- Other stuff as you desire. This can be darn near anything you like, such as cut-up peppers, zucchini, chicken, bacon, various cheeses, salmon, spinach, kale, cooked potatoes... you get the idea. All of it should be pre-cooked, so this is a great way to use up leftovers.

Utensils
- Iron skillet (you can also use a 2-quart, oven-proof baking dish)

Step 1: Pour the oil into the skillet and cook the onions for about 5 minutes. Set skillet aside with onions in it.

Step 2: In a bowl, mix the eggs, milk, salt and pepper.

Step 3: Add the "other stuff" to the skillet, followed by the egg mixture. Stir gently to mix it. Then return the skillet to the heat and cook for about 5 to 7 minutes, until the edges start to pull away from the pan.

Step 4: Remove skillet from stove and place in oven at 350° until set, about 16-18 minutes.

You'll want some good oven mitts or pot holders when making this recipe.

Is it Raw or Hard Boiled?

Spin the egg in question. If it spins pretty well on end, it is a hard-boiled egg. If it doesn't spin too well and wobbles, it is a raw egg. Try spinning a raw egg and very briefly touching it, just long enough to stop it. When you take your finger away, the egg will start to spin slightly more. This is due to the inertia of the liquid egg inside.

Mustard Potato Salad

Ingredients
- 2 cups salad dressing or mayo
- ½ cup sugar
- 1 Tablespoon yellow mustard
- ½ cup celery, chopped
- ½ cup onion, chopped
- 4 - 6 potatoes, peeled, cooked, cooled, sliced
- 4 hard-boiled eggs, sliced
- Paprika
- Parsley
- Salt and pepper to taste

Step 1: Combine salad dressing, sugar and mustard. Mix in celery and onions. Add sliced potatoes and 2 sliced eggs. Salt and pepper to taste.

Step 2: Put into serving bowl and garnish with other 2 eggs, paprika and parsley. Chill several hours or overnight before serving.

HAM & EGG MASH-UPS

Ingredients
- 1 cup mashed potatoes
- ¼ cup ham, chopped
- ¼ cup cheddar cheese
- ¼ cup sour cream
- 1 Tablespoon green onion tops, chopped
- 2 eggs
- Salt & pepper to taste

You can substitute ¼ cup French onion chip dip for the sour cream and green onions.

Utensils
- 2 ramekins (individual-sized baking dishes)

Step 1: Mix together the mashed potatoes, sour cream, green onions, ham and cheese.

Step 2: Mold half of the mixture into each of the ramekins, leaving a large indent in the center. Bake at 375° for about 20 minutes, until edges begin to crisp.

Step 3: Remove from oven and crack an egg into each ramekin, salt and pepper to taste, then return it to oven for another 15 to 20 minutes, until eggs are set.

A typical hen lays an average of 266 eggs per year. The record is 371 eggs in one year.

Spamwich Spread

Ingredients
- 1 can Spam or similar canned meat, ground
- ¼ cup finely chopped onion
- 3 raw carrots, grated
- 6 hard-boiled eggs, chopped
- 1 stalk celery, chopped
- ¼ cup pickle relish
- 1 cup cut-in-half grapes
- 1 cup salad dressing or mayo
- 2 Tablespoons sugar
- 2 Tablespoons vinegar
- 1 teaspoon salt

This recipe makes enough spread for a dozen or more sandwiches so you can feed the whole family.

Step 1: Mix together Spam, onion, carrots, eggs and celery. Add remaining ingredients and mix well. Refrigerate for an hour before serving.

Spinach Bacon Salad

Ingredients
- 1 bunch or bag of washed spinach
- 1 can sliced water chestnuts
- 1 can bean sprouts
- 2 hard-boiled eggs

Dressing
- ½ pound bacon
- ¼ cup vinegar
- ⅓ cup ketchup
- 1 onion, chopped fine
- ¾ cup sugar
- ¾ cup oil
- 2 Tablespoons Worcestershire sauce

Step 1: Toss together spinach, chestnuts and bean sprouts. Set aside.

Step 2: Fry bacon and onion, drain. Add rest of dressing ingredients to bacon mixture and simmer 15 minutes.

Step 3: Pour dressing over salad, garnish with eggs, serve immediately.

Need Some Emergency Glue?

Egg protein becomes incredibly tacky when dry, forming a sticky sealant that will rival Elmer's. If you run out of traditional glue, just whisk up some egg whites and use the solution to bond paper, light cardboard or even seal a papier-mache project together.

Pickled Beets and Eggs

Ingredients
- 1 can (15 oz. each) whole beets
- 6 hard-boiled eggs, peeled
- ½ cup sugar
- ½ cup water
- ½ cup cider vinegar

These are fun because the eggs turn purple, with bright yellow centers.

Utensils
- 1-quart wide-mouth glass jar with lid

Step 1: Drain the beets, saving ½ cup of the juice.

Step 2: Place beets and eggs in the 1-quart glass jar.

Step 3: In a saucepan, bring the sugar, water, vinegar and half cup of saved beet juice to a boil. Pour over beets and eggs.

Step 4: When cool, cover tightly and refrigerate. Wait at least 24 hours before serving. Use within a week.

Q: Where is the best place to learn about eggs?

A: In the hen-cyclopedia

The Fox and the Little Red Hen

Once upon a time there was a little red hen. She lived in a little white house, and she had a little green garden. Every day she worked in the house and garden.

Near her home lived a family of foxes. One day Mamma Fox said to Papa Fox, "There is nothing in the pantry for the baby foxes," so Papa Fox started out to find something for them to eat.

He ran down the road until he came to the woods. "Surely I will find something here," he said, but he found nothing to eat in the woods. As he came near the little green garden he said, "Oh, I smell fresh cake. Oh, I smell a little red hen."

Sure enough, there was the Little Red Hen eating her cake.

Papa Fox snuck up quietly behind her and grabbed her and put her into the bag on his back; then he ran quickly off down the hill toward his home.

The Little Red Hen was so frightened that she could only whisper, "Oh, dear. Oh, dear. Oh, dear."

Just then she had to sneeze, and when she put her claw into her pocket for her handkerchief, she felt her little scissors. Quick as a flash she took them out and cut a little hole in the bag. Peeping out she saw a great hill just ahead, all covered with stones. As Papa Fox stopped to rest on his way up the hill, with his back turned toward her, she cut a larger hole in the bag, jumped out and quickly put a big stone in the bag in her place.

As Papa Fox kept on up the hill, he thought the bag was pretty heavy, but he said, "Never mind, she is a fat little red hen."

Mamma Fox met him at the front door with all the baby foxes.

"The water is boiling," said she.

"What have you in your bag?" asked the Baby Foxes.

"A fat, little, red hen," said Papa Fox.

As he held the bag over the pot, he said to Mamma Fox, "When I drop her in, you clap on the lid." So he opened the bag. Splash! went the boiling water. It spilled all over Papa Fox and Mamma Fox and the Baby Foxes. Never again did they try to catch the Little Red Hen.

Craizy Banana Applesauce Bread

Ingredients
- 4 ripe bananas
- 1 cup sugar
- ½ cup applesauce
- 3 oz. craisins (about ⅓ cup)
- 2 eggs
- 1 teaspoon baking soda
- 1 Tablespoon baking powder
- 1 teaspoon salt
- 1 teaspoon vanilla extract
- 2 cups flour

Go wild and add ½ cup of nuts and maybe some shredded carrots!

Step 1: Mash bananas, stir in sugar. Let sit for 10 to 15 minutes.

Step 2: Add the remaining ingredients, mixing well. Pour into two oiled loaf pans.

Step 3: Bake at 375° for about 50 minutes, until a toothpick poked into the center comes out clean.

Step 4: Let cool for 10 minutes, then remove from pan.

Zucchini Bread

Ingredients
- Butter and flour for preparing baking pans
- 3 cups all-purpose flour
- 1 teaspoon salt
- 1 teaspoon baking soda
- 1 teaspoon baking powder
- 4 teaspoons ground cinnamon
- 3½ cups grated zucchini
- 3 eggs
- ½ cup apple sauce
- ½ cup vegetable oil
- 2¼ cups granulated sugar
- 4 teaspoons vanilla extract
- 1 cup chopped pecans

Utensils
- 2 bread pans

Step 1: Preheat oven to 350 degrees F. Generously butter and lightly flour two 8"x 4" loaf pans.

Step 2: In a medium bowl, blend together flour, salt, baking soda, baking powder and cinnamon.

Step 3: In a larger bowl, beat together the eggs, applesauce, oil, sugar and vanilla extract. Slowly add the dry ingredients, mixing well.

Step 4: Stir shredded zucchini and nuts into the batter and mix well. Pour half the batter into each pan.

Step 5: Bake at 350° for 45 to 60 minutes or until a toothpick inserted into the center of the loaf comes out cleanly.

Baking time will vary depending on the moisture content of the zucchini.

Fried Rice & Shrimp

Ingredients
- 4 cups rice, precooked
- ½ pound bacon
- 2 eggs
- 1 cup peas and carrots (thawed, if frozen)
- ½ cup chopped green onions
- 1 cup small cooked shrimp
- Soy sauce to taste

Shrimp can be replaced with cubed, cooked chicken.

Step 1: In a large skillet, fry bacon until crisp, remove from pan, and set aside. When cool, break up the bacon.

Step 2: In the same pan, scramble eggs in bacon drippings. Without removing from heat, mix in peas, carrots, green onions, bacon, cooked shrimp and cooked rice. Continue cooking at medium temp about 10 minutes, until heated through. Add soy sauce to taste.

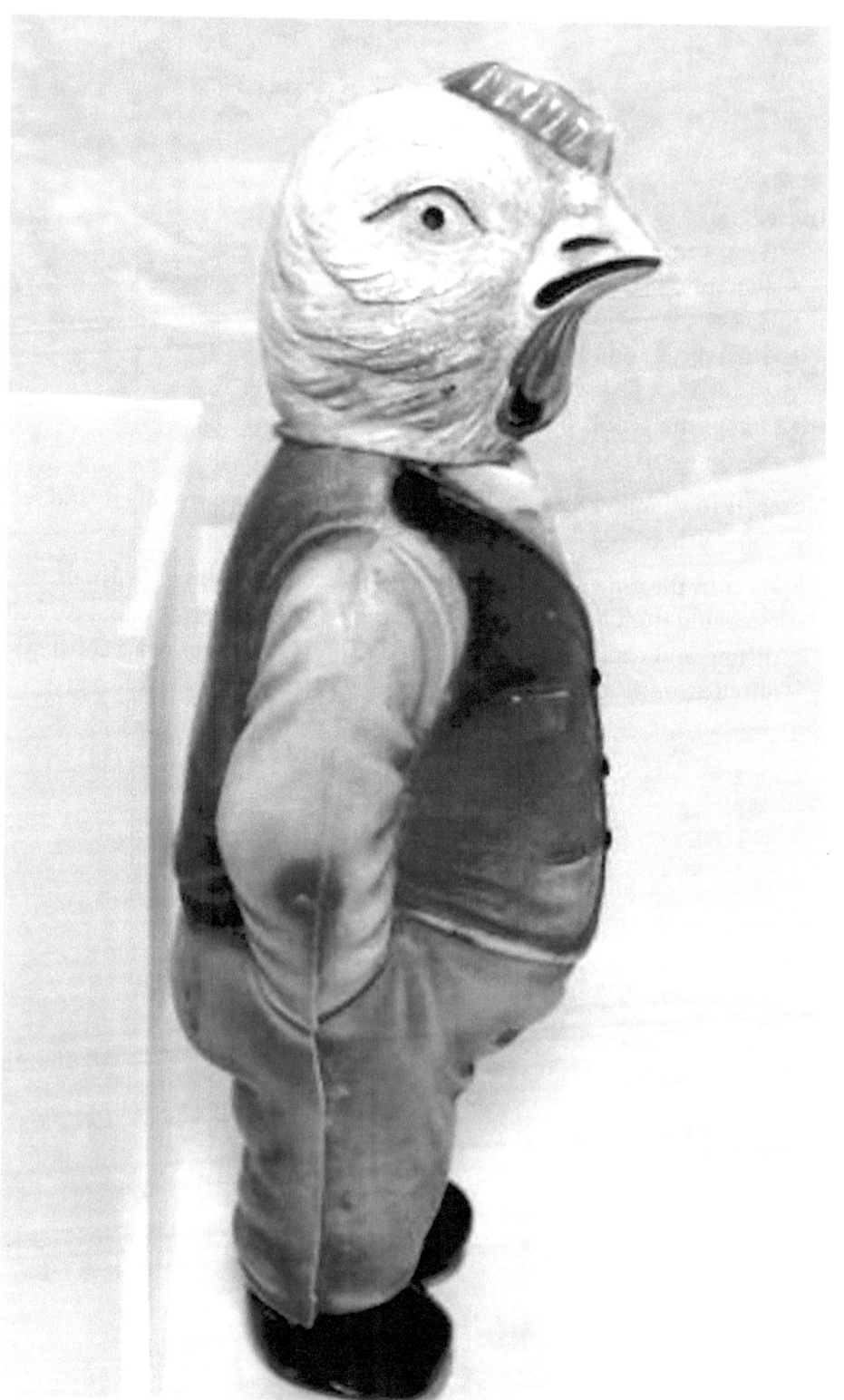

BAKED CUSTARD

Ingredients
- 4 eggs
- ⅓ cup sugar
- ¼ teaspoon salt
- 3 cups hot milk
- 1 teaspoon vanilla
- Nutmeg (as desired)

Utensils
- Custard cups (4 large or 6 small)
- A baking pan that will hold all of the custard cups

Appliances
- Oven preheated to 325°

Step 1: Combine the eggs, sugar and salt. Stir in the milk gradually. Add vanilla.

Step 2: Pour into custard cups. Sprinkle with nutmeg. Set cups into a pan that has about an inch of hot water.

Step 3: Bake at 325° for 30 to 40 minutes; until the tip of a knife inserted in the center comes out clean.

Serve either warm or cold, depending on your preference.

Note to self: When moving the water-filled pan, be careful to keep the pot holders dry... heat goes through a wet pot holder very quickly!

The platypus both lays eggs and produces milk, making it one of the few animals that can make its own custard.

Q: Why do chickens rinse their mouth out with soap?

A: Because of all the fowl language.

Lemon Meringue Pie

Ingredients
- 9" deep-dish pie shell, prebaked

Filling
- ½ cup cornstarch
- 1 cup sugar
- ½ cup lemon juice
- 1 ¼ cup water
- 2 teaspoons lemon zest (grated lemon peel)
- 4 egg yolks
- 4 tablespoons butter, room temperature

Meringue
- 4 egg whites, room temperature
- ½ cup sugar

This recipe uses 4 eggs. Separate the yolks from the whites when you start, so they're ready when needed.

Step 1: Bake pie shell according to your favorite recipe or package instructions, then remove from oven to cool. Reset oven to 375°.

Step 2: Combine cornstarch, sugar, lemon juice, water and lemon zest in cooking pan and stir until smooth. Cook over medium heat, stirring constantly until it boils. Remove from heat.

Step 3: Mix together the egg yolks and butter, then stir them into the mixture in the cooking pan. Return it to the heat and, stirring constantly, bring it back to a boil until it thickens, which may happen quickly. Don't let it scorch. When thick, set aside.

Step 4: When filling has cooled a bit, fill prebaked pastry crust.

Step 5: In a clean mixing bowl, beat the egg whites, adding the sugar a little at a time, until stiff peaks form.

Step 6: Using a spatula, spread the meringue over the lemon filling, pulling the spatula up to make the peaks. Be sure that it touches the edges of the crust or it will shrink to the middle when baked.

Step 7: Bake at 375° about 10 minutes or until meringue is golden.

A wire whisk supposedly can be used to whip egg whites, but an electric mixer works much, much better. Blenders and food processors won't do the job. Avoid using plastic or wooden mixing bowls as the oil in them keeps the peaks from forming easily. For the stiffest peaks, add 1/8 teaspoon of cream of tarter for each egg white.

Meringue or Merengue?

Meringue is a tasty confection made from sugar and whipped egg whites that you can enjoy as a dessert topping. **Merengue**, on the other hand, is a lively Latin dance. Be careful which you choose to put on top of your lemon pie.

Strawberry Honey Omelette

Ingredients
- 4 eggs, separated
- Salt & pepper to taste
- 2 Tablespoons butter, melted, divided
- 1 cup fresh strawberries
- 1 Tablespoon honey
- Powdered sugar

Utensils
- Microwavable 10" pie plate

Step 1: In medium mixing bowl, beat egg whites until stiff but not dry.

Step 2: In separate bowl, beat egg yolks, salt and pepper until thickened. Fold egg yokes into egg whites and carefully pour the mixture into a microwavable pie pan that is heavily buttered with the first Tablespoon of melted butter.

Step 3: Microwave at HIGH for 1 to 2 minutes. Turn ¼ turn and microwave at HIGH another 1 to 2 minutes. Let stand for two minutes, then with a spatula, loosen the edges of the omelette from the pie plate.

Step 4: Mix strawberries, honey and the remaining Tablespoon of melted butter. Spoon into half of the omelette and fold over. Sprinkle with powdered sugar as desired.

Sunny Lemon Squares

Ingredients
- 2 ½ cups flour, divided
- 1 cup (2 sticks) butter, softened
- 1 cup powdered sugar, plus extra for topping
- 4 cups granulated sugar
- 4 eggs
- 1 teaspoon lemon extract

Step 1: Preheat oven to 350°.

Step 2: Mix 2 cups flour, butter and 1 cup powdered sugar until crumbly. Press into bottom of a 9" x 13" baking pan to form a crust. Bake at 350° about 15 minutes.

Step 3: In a large bowl, with an electric mixer on medium speed, beat remaining ½ cup flour, granulated sugar, eggs, lemon juice and lemon extract until well blended. Pour over hot crust.

Step 4: Bake at 350° for 25 to 30 minutes or until set.

Step 5: Allow to cool and cut into squares. Dust with powdered sugar and serve.

Q: Why did the chicken stop in the middle of the road?

A: Because it wanted to lay it on the line.

Use Egg Whites to Clean Leather

Egg whites are delicate enough to polish your skin but hardy enough to fight stains on leather too. To remove surface blemishes, gently scrub an egg white solution onto old leather-- any color-- and wipe off with a dampened cloth. Not only will the wash lift off old stains, the protein will form a protective barrier from future damage.

Mile High Pound Cake

Ingredients
- 4 cups flour
- 1 teaspoon baking powder
- 4 cups sugar
- ¼ cup lemon juice
- ½ teaspoon salt
- 2 cups butter at room temperature
- 10 eggs at room temperature

Utensils
- Tube pan

Step 1: Preheat oven to 325°. Grease and lightly flour bottom of tube pan.

Step 2: Sift together flour, baking powder and salt.

Step 3: Cream butter. Gradually add sugar, beating all the time. Beat in eggs, one at a time.

Step 4: Add dry ingredients. Beat. Add lemon juice. Pour batter into prepared pan.

Step 5: Bake for 1 hour and 45 minutes to 2 hours or until done. Check with a toothpick. Cool on a wire rack. Serves 12.

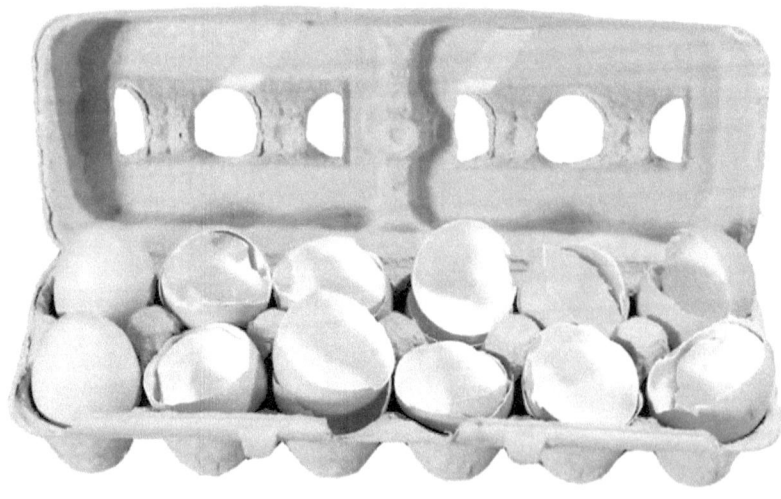

Classic Lemon Curd

Ingredients
- ¾ cup fresh lemon juice
- 1 Tablespoon grated lemon zest
- ¾ cup granulated sugar
- 3 eggs
- ½ cup butter, cubed

Perfect topping for the Mile High Pound Cake.

Step 1: In a 2-quart saucepan, combine lemon juice, lemon zest, sugar, eggs and butter.

Step 2: Cook over medium-low heat until thick enough to hold marks from whisk and first bubbles appear on the surface, about 6 minutes.

Step 3: Remove from heat.

Step 4: Put into a refrigerator container and press plastic wrap onto the surface to keep the skin from forming on top. Curd will thicken as it cools. Keep refrigerated and use within a week.

Eggs and Early Photography

Many of the older pictures in this book were originally created using eggs! Called albumen silver prints, the method used the albumen found in egg whites to bind the photographic chemicals to the paper. It was the most common method of making photographic prints from 1855 to the turn of the 20th century.

Hummingbird Cake

Ingredients
- 1 package yellow cake mix
- 1 package vanilla instant pudding and pie filling
- ½ cup vegetable oil
- 1 (8 oz.) can crushed pineapple, well drained (save the juice)
- 4 eggs
- 1 teaspoon ground cinnamon
- 1 ripe banana, cut up
- ½ cup finely chopped pecans
- ¼ cup chopped maraschino cherries, drained
- ⅓ cup prepared cream cheese frosting

Utensils
- 10" Bundt pan, coated with cooking spray

Step 1: Combine the cake and pudding mixes, the oil, pineapple, eggs and cinnamon. Add enough water to the saved pineapple juice to make 1 cup; add it to bowl then beat with an electric mixer until thoroughly combined.

Step 2: Stir in banana, pecans and cherries, mix well with a spatula, then pour into prepared pan.

Step 3: Bake at 350° for 55 to 60 minutes, or until a toothpick inserted in the center comes out clean.

Step 4: Let cake cool in pan about 20 minutes, then invert onto a serving plate. Once cooled completely, drizzle warmed frosting over cake before slicing.

The Cock and the Fox

One bright evening, as the sun was sinking on a glorious world, a wise old Cock flew into a tree to roost. Before he composed himself to rest, he flapped his wings three times and crowed loudly. But just as he was about to put his head under his wing, his beady eyes caught a flash of red and a glimpse of a long pointed nose, and there just below him stood Master Fox.

"Have you heard the wonderful news?" cried the Fox in a very joyful and excited manner.

"What news?" asked the Cock very calmly. But he had a strange, fluttery feeling inside him, for, you know, he was very much afraid of the Fox.

"Your family and mine and all other animals have agreed to forget their differences and live in peace and friendship from now on forever," said the Fox. "Just think of it! I simply cannot wait to embrace you! Do come down, dear friend, and let us celebrate the joyful event."

"How grand!" said the Cock. "I certainly am delighted at the news." But he spoke in an absent way, and stretching up on tiptoes, seemed to be looking at something afar off.

"What is it you see?" asked the Fox a little anxiously.

"Why, it looks to me like a couple of Dogs coming this way. They must have heard the good news and—"

But the Fox did not wait to hear more. Off he started on a run.

"Wait," cried the Cock. "Why do you run? The Dogs are friends of yours now!"

"Yes," answered the Fox. "But they might not have heard the news. Besides, I have a very important errand that I had almost forgotten about."

The Cock smiled as he buried his head in his feathers and went to sleep, for he had succeeded in outwitting a very crafty enemy.

The trickster is easily tricked.

"I train in the mornings, and I'll eat two breakfasts. I'll have waffles with flax seed and almond butter and one egg scrambled. Then I'll work out and have a second breakfast - another egg or a protein shake. Within a half-hour to 40 minutes after a workout, that's when you want to load up on protein."

—Justin Timberlake

Bread Pudding

Ingredients
- 6 slices day-old bread
- 2 Tablespoons butter, melted
- ½ cup raisins (optional)
- 4 eggs, beaten
- 2 cups milk
- ¾ cup white sugar
- 1 teaspoon ground cinnamon
- 1 teaspoon vanilla extract

Step 1: Break bread into small pieces in an 8" baking pan. Drizzle melted butter over bread and sprinkle with raisins, if desired.

Step 2: In a mixing bowl, beat together eggs, milk, sugar, cinnamon and vanilla. Pour over bread, pushing down the bread to make sure it is covered with the egg/milk mixture.

Step 3: Bake at 350° for about 45 minutes, until the top springs back when lightly tapped.

Congo Bars

Ingredients
- 2 ½ cups brown sugar
- ⅔ cup oil
- 3 eggs
- 2 ½ cups flour
- 1 ½ teaspoons baking powder
- 1 teaspoon vanilla
- 1 small pkg. (6 oz.) chocolate chips
- 1 cup coconut

Pecans are often also included in the mixture.

Step 1: Mix together all ingredients. Press into a 9" x 13" pan. Bake at 350° for about 30 to 35 minutes.

Old-Fashioned Blueberry Muffins

Ingredients
- 2 cups flour
- ½ cup sugar
- 3 teaspoons baking powder
- ½ teaspoon salt
- 1 teaspoon grated lemon or orange peel
- 1 cup blueberries (if frozen, do not thaw)
- ¾ cup milk
- ⅓ cup oil
- 1 egg

Take a few fresh blueberries out to your chickens. They'll love you forever!

Utensils
- Muffin tin with paper baking cups (12)

Step 1: Combine flour, sugar, baking powder, salt and lemon/orange peel; mix well. Gently stir in blueberries.

Step 2: In a small bowl, mix together milk, oil and egg. Add to dry ingredients and stir until uniform consistency.

Step 3: Fill muffin papers ⅔ full. Bake at 400° for 25 to 30 minutes, until light golden brown.

Homemade Tom & Jerry Eggnog

Ingredients
- 6 large eggs
- 1 cup sugar
- 2 cups milk
- 1 cup heavy cream
- Pinch of ground allspice
- Pinch of ground cinnamon
- Pinch of ground cloves
- 4 oz. brandy, rum or combination
- Grated nutmeg, to serve

This can also be made without the brandy or rum for a nonalcoholic eggnog.

Step 1: Separate the eggs, placing the yolks in one bowl and the whites in another. Cover the whites and set aside until needed (see Step 4).

Step 2: Whisk together the yolks and the sugar until smooth and creamy. Then whisk in the milk, cream, rum and spices.

Step 3: Refrigerate for at least an hour before serving.

Step 4: To serve, beat the egg whites until it forms stiff peaks, then fold the beaten egg whites into the eggnog. Sprinkle with nutmeg.

> NOTE: This recipe uses raw eggs. If you are using eggs from your backyard chickens, they are most likely safe, but err on the side of caution and use only eggs that are fresh, clean and have no cracks.

The Tom and Jerry was created in the 1850s by Jerry Thomas at the Planters' House Hotel, St. Louis.

Flour-Free Monster Cookies

Ingredients
- 4 eggs
- 1 heaping cup brown sugar
- 1 cup white sugar
- ½ cup butter
- 1 ½ cup peanut butter
- 2 teaspoons baking soda
- 4 ½ cups quick oats
- ½ cup M&Ms
- 1 teaspoon vanilla
- 1 cup chocolate chips
- ½ cup chopped nuts

Step 1: In a large bowl, mix together eggs, brown sugar, white sugar and butter.

Step 2: Add rest of ingredients to previous mixture, blending well.

Step 3: Place on greased cookie sheet according to the size you want. Bake at 350° for 12 to 15 minutes. Larger cookies will take longer to bake. Do not overbake.

*To keep the cookies from breaking,
let cool on cookie sheet before removing them.*

Equivalent Weights & Measures

- 1 pound of butter = 2 cups
- 1 stick of butter = ½ cup
- 2 cups sugar = 1 pound
- 2 ½ cups packed brown sugar = 1 pound
- 4 cups sifted all purpose flour = 1 pound
- 1 cup egg whites = 8 to 10 whites
- 1 cup egg yolks = 12 to 14 yolks
- 10 graham crackers = 1 cup fine crumbs
- 1 cup whipping cream = 2 cups whipped
- 1 lemon = 3 to 4 tablespoons juice

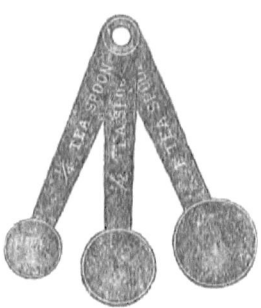

- 3 teaspoons = 1 Tablespoon
- 2 Tablespoons = 1 fluid ounce
- 4 Tablespoons = ¼ cup
- 5 ⅓ Tablespoons = ⅓ cup
- 1 cup = ½ pint
- 2 cups = 1 pint
- 4 cups = 1 quart

It's my first day on the fishing boat and everyone keeps asking if I've found my sea legs. I'm not falling for it, though. I know for a fact that seals don't lay eggs.

Tips for Decorating & Dying Eggs

● You can make your own egg dye by adding 25 drops of food coloring to ½ cup of boiling water and ½ teaspoon of white vinegar.

● Before you dye the egg, use a white crayon to write names or draw designs on the egg. The wax resists the dye, so whatever you draw on the egg turns out to be the original egg color. Dry the egg and you can do this again and the first color will remain where you put the wax.

● You can create bands of color by sticking narrow strips of masking tape around the egg. For a fun surprise pattern, dry the egg and keep adding more strips and dipping it into different colors until the egg is covered with tape. The tape can also be cut into shapes. When dry, remove the tape.

The most expensive egg ever sold was the 1913 Fabergé Winter Egg, which sold in 1994 for $5.6 million and again in 2002 for $9.6 million.

How to Suck an Egg Inside a Milk Bottle

Needed:
- 1 hard-boiled egg
- 1 glass milk bottle (A Starbucks bottle will also work)

Step 1: Use a paper towel to coat the inside edge of the bottle mouth with a little bit of vegetable oil for lubrication.

Step 2: Dip the egg in water and set it with the small end down in the mouth of the glass bottle. It should be slightly larger than the mouth of the bottle, so it doesn't fit inside.

Step 3: Use a match to light the end of a strip of paper on fire. Lift the egg off the bottle, drop the paper inside with the flame down, and quickly replace the egg. Watch the egg wiggle a little in the bottle mouth, and then get sucked inside! When we tried it, the pressure was so strong that the egg was crushed!

Rubber Eggy Bubbly Bouncer

Needed:
- An egg, either raw or hard boiled
- A tall drinking glass or wide-mouth glass jar
- White vinegar

Step 1: Put your egg into a tall drinking glass.

Step 2: Pour vinegar into the glass until the egg is covered. Set the glass aside so no one drinks and/or spills it. Ignore the vinegar smell. Let the egg soak overnight. You should notice a lot of foam and bubbles.

Step 3: The next day, rinse the vinegar and foam out with water and then cover the egg again with vinegar. Wait for six days.

Step 4: At the end of this time, rinse off the egg and pick it up. It will feel different than when you started... most noticeably it is missing the shell and has a weird rubbery feel to it. Shake it. Gently squeeze it.

Test out your rubber egg in the sink by dropping it from a few inches and then from a little higher.

With a **raw egg**, the effect is more fun, but if it breaks it will make a mess. With a **hard-boiled egg**, it mostly feels like a rubbery version of a hard-boiled egg without a shell.

I'm always bending the neighbors' ears about things I learned while tending our sweet little flock. Eggbert convinced me to write them down so he could put them in his little book. I hope you enjoy reading them. If not, blame Eggbert.

—*Henrietta Fowler*

Always Count Your Chickens After They've Hatched

Sometimes Eggbert lets the chickens run around the yard. They enjoy it, but it's extra work for me. Each night after they've gone in to roost I have to close up the coop so some hungry varmint doesn't come in for a late-night snack.

One drizzly evening my lumbago was acting up, so I sent Eggbert out to close up the henhouse, which he did just fine, but he got lazy and didn't check that everyone was present and accounted for. Our ladies should not be gallivanting around at all hours of the night.

The next morning, we discovered that Cleo, our oldest hen, had spent a wet night under our back porch. I believe she and Eggbert both learned their lesson: Always count your chickens.

New Kids on the Block

When our first little flock was three years old, we decided to add some youngsters to the mix. The local farmer's store had their annual chick days and the sweet young woman behind the counter assured us that the day-old chicks we selected were little girls. We kept them in the garage under a heat lamp for the first few weeks, giving them lots of attention and hand feeding them.

When they outgrew the tub in the garage, we decided to introduce them to the others. The trick was to keep them safe. Eggbert dug out the wire kennel we used for our dog when traveling. We put the youngsters in the kennel, then set it, with its own water and feed, in the run.

When everyone seemed to be getting used to each other, we opened the door to the kennel. The kids used it as their own little playhouse for awhile and stayed out of the old hens' way. After a couple days, we removed the kennel. There were a few lessons about pecking order, and at first, the youngsters stayed in their own little group, but it wasn't long before everyone was getting along fine.

A Pullet is a Baby Hen, Right?

Remember those three chicks that the sweet young woman at the farmer's store said were little girls. Well, they were growing unusually large combs and getting pretty snitty with each other. Ollie, our rooster, had to break up their spats more than once. When they started taking after the hens, Ollie stepped in to protect his girls in no uncertain terms. The old fellow was getting worn down from always being on guard.

We finally offered the pullets-turned-roosters to our neighbors. We never asked what they did with them, but a couple days later they fired up the grills for a big family picnic.

Something to Crow About

Speaking of roosters. If you live in town, there's probably a rule forbidding you from having one. Thinking from a neighbor's perspective at 5 a.m., that's a pretty good idea.

We live in the country and Ollie crows every morning. Also in the middle of the day. Even at night, if he thinks there's something prowling around the coop.

His crowing makes a pretty good burglar alarm, too. When a car pulls into the driveway, he often crows to alert us. He also crows if he wants fresh water or a treat.

If you're in the henhouse and he crows right next to your ear, it's like being in a church steeple when the bells ring. Good golly he's got a set of pipes on him.

An Officer and a Gentleman

When it comes to his ladies, Ollie is a gentleman. If we bring them a treat, he lets his girls start snacking before he takes any himself.

He's their protector, too. If a hawk flies over, he make a sound that causes the hens to freeze in place. When the hawk is out of sight, he scoots them all inside the coop.

When we put new bedding in the nesting boxes, he always checks to make sure everything is in order, pulling out pieces of straw that hang over the edge.

He never goes in the boxes himself, but he wants them in good shape for his girls.

Sometimes he gets a bit rambunctious with his girls, if you know what I mean, and he does tend to play favorites. But if a hen isn't interested, she usually lets him know and he seems to respect her wishes... at least for a few minutes.

A couple times Ollie decided that I was the intruder and puffed out his chest and charged me. It ended when I decided to charge him back.

Blueberries & Wonder Bread

Our chickens are pets and we're not too proud to spoil them. When we collect the eggs, we often take them a treat. Their favorite snack is blueberries (as long as there's a really, really good sale). They don't like strawberries.

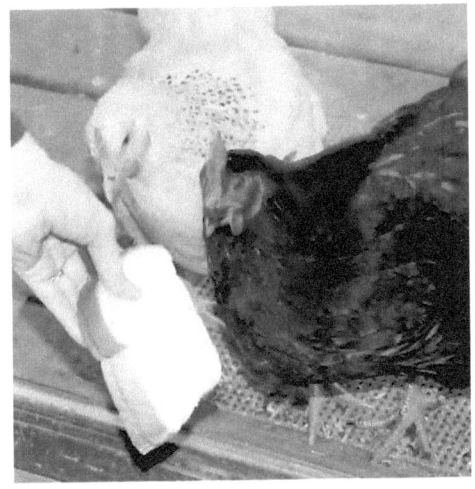

Next highest on the list is white bread. They'll come running when they see us walking toward them with a slice in our hand. Corn bread is a big hit, too. And they adore leftover French fries and tater tots.

They do a great job of cleaning up our kitchen leftovers. But they won't eat everything. We gave them some canned Italian-flavored tomatoes once. Each, in turn, took a taste, made the same "that's disgusting" sound and proceeded to wipe their beaks on the ground. We didn't like the stuff, either, which is why we offered it to them.

Chicken Feed vs Chicken Feed

For the first two years, we bought the exact same layer feed at the farm supply store. It was cheap and they ate it without complaining. Then a woman a couple towns over, who had hundreds of chickens, recommended that we try some non-GMO custom feed from the local mill.

The chickens not only liked the new stuff better, but tossed all of the remaining old feed on the floor to get to it. It was apparently better for their health, too. One of our old hens, who had stopped laying several months before we switched feed, started laying again, and her eggs were even bigger than before.

The Award Goes to Bohemian Rhapsody

One day we had company over for lunch and the guests wanted to see our chickens, so we tossed a few treats out on the back porch. The always-curious flock pecked away while watching us through the patio door.

Our dinner music that day was Queen, turned up to a reasonable volume, and when Brian May broke into his guitar solo on "Bohemian Rhapsody" all of the chickens stopped eating, pressed up against the glass, heads cocked, and listened attentively, bopping along to the music. When the song ended, it was back to pecking, same as before.

Who is Gazing at Whom?

Our kitchen window looks out directly at the henhouse and I often find myself watching Ollie and the girls as I prepare supper. Just as often, I notice that they are lined up along the side of the run watching me. I can just imagine them telling each other, "Hey look, the old hen just turned on the light." "Maybe she's getting a snack for us." "I hope it's blueberries!"

The Pied Piper

When it comes to snacks, Eggbert is a soft touch. A few happy clucks and he's heading to the run with a handful of their favorite seeds. They know this. And it's really funny to watch, because if the chickens are out and my dear sweet husband is working in the yard, they follow him around like the Pied Piper, knowing full well that he'll reward them for looking cute.

Bring Out the Broom

We enjoy the chickens company, but we don't like them pooping all over the deck. I discovered that I could chase them away with a couple gentle swats of my broom. It didn't take long before all I had to do was pick up the broom and they'd leave. To keep them off the deck when I wasn't there, I'd lay the broom across the top of the steps.

On the Outside Looking In

Star is our adventurous red hen. She's the first one out of the coop when it's opened up for the day. When Eggbert was building a new gate for an extended, uncovered run (he calls it their playpen), Star stayed with him the whole time, watching what he was doing, while the others hid in the henhouse, nervous about the pounding and sawing.

The fence on the playpen is only four feet tall. Of course Star had to fly over it. The others stayed inside. After a few hours of this, she was quite distraught to be outside alone, pacing back and forth along the fence perimeter. When Eggbert picked her up, she snuggled up to him like he'd rescued her from disaster. Ollie gave her a bit of a scolding when she was returned to the pen. Two days later, she "escaped" again, with the same results. Even though she can easily get out, that was the last time she flew the coop.

www.ingramcontent.com/pod-product-compliance
Lightning Source LLC
Chambersburg PA
CBHW021132300426
44113CB00006B/396